Infinity: Overcoming 1

By Craig Beck

The free companion downloads for these books are available to download at www.craigbeck.com

Chapters

Introduction

Birth and death are the only two events that we all share. One is remembered and acknowledged every year and is considered a joyful celebration. The other we bury deep in our subconscious and never talk of it. We don't just forget that we are going to die, but rather, most of us spend a lifetime passively terrified by the mere thought of it.

Death is coming to us all and it's doesn't care how much money or status you have. As the saying goes 'nobody is getting out of this alive', so if you want to ever be truly at peace in this lifetime, the first and most important step is to accept your eventual death, as readily as you do your birth.

Western society has stuck its head in the sand and prefers the universal pretense that death doesn't really exist; it is just something that happens to other people. Our every dealing with it is sanitized. We don't even like to talk about people dying, instead we dilute it by referring to it as passing on etc. We don't talk about it and we don't accept it, because for most people, the thought of the end is our biggest and most horrific fear.

In this profound and life shifting book, new thought author Craig Beck, takes on this most taboo of subjects. He shows you why you have nothing to be afraid of and how you can find peace in the knowledge and acceptance of death. Not just of those who you share your life with, but also the thought of ultimately, your own death.

Discover:

- The power of now – living in the moment.
- Limitless mindset and potential.
- The reassurances revealed by palliative care nurses.
- Peace and happiness beyond your dreams.
- Healing rifts and problem relationships.
- Living life to your full potential.
- The peace revealed by Near Death Experiences.
- Understanding and coping with death and grief.

While many people will avoid this book, due entirely to the subject matter. Those who are brave enough to take the journey will discover a whole new level of peace, purpose and happiness.

www.CraigBeck.com

Chapter One – 28th August 2001 Darlington, England

"I do not fear death. I had been dead for billions and billions of years before I was born, and had not suffered the slightest inconvenience from it." Mark Twain

Something strange had happened in England, nobody could quite understand why, but briefly for a few hours it appeared to have stopped raining. The whole of the male population of the United Kingdom rushed en masse to their sheds and garages, for it was at last a chance to put the rusting and dust covered BBQ to some use. There is nothing us men like better than poking meat with a stick, over an over enthusiastically primed fire. It's quite a peculiar thing, even the most culinary challenged man believes that when he is behind the grill he has the standards and technique of Gordon Ramsey. In many respects I am quite a sensitive, metrosexual sort of man. I do not go weak at the knees when a flashy car goes past me. I have no desire to tinker with any sort of engine and I can't stand soccer! However, as much as I take pride in my connection to my feminine side, I still get the caveman style urge to poke a fire when I see one. How disappointingly predictable I know, but there you go and that is exactly what I was doing when the telephone rang at 6pm on 28th August 2001.

My wife opened the kitchen window and called out to me that my brother was on the phone. This in itself was worrying, because he never calls me and in the interest of honesty I also never call him. Please don't think that we had some big falling out, or don't see eye to eye on some important issues. We are both just ridiculously poor at staying in touch with each other. We have allowed this distance to become the norm and now, when one of us does attempt some sort of communication, the instant reaction from the other sibling is one of shock, worry and suspicion. So when the phone rings and it is my brother, I tend to get the same sort of feeling that most people get when their partner looks them in the eye and says' 'we need to talk'!

I complained briefly about my exceptional standards of steak grilling being compromised by the interruption and made my way into the house to take the call.

"What's up, is your computer broken again? That's the only time you ever call me little brother", I said, laughing.

"Granddad is dead", my brother Mark replied, in a voice that failed to hide how much deep breathing he had had to do, to utter that sentence without allowing his voice to crack.

"Oh, erm right, thank you for letting me know", I said, as stiff and as devoid of emotion as a plank of wood. In truth, the call ended before the reality of what he had just said had even registered. I stood staring at the phone for what felt like hours, but it must have been no more than thirty seconds before my wife shouted through from the kitchen and I was dragged back into the real world.

"The steaks are burning Mr. Caveman", my wife shouted. I walked to the BBQ and stood watching the meat burn, before finally saying 'my Granddad is dead'.

Granddad John Prest, who everyone called Jack for short. Yes, I know what your thinking and to this day I still don't know how Jack is short for John, but that's another story. The point is, he was my absolute hero, something I am telling you, but I am sad to say that I never got the chance to tell him personally when he was alive. You see my father ran his own business, a butchers shop in the Darlington Covered Market. He worked so hard on that business that he had already been at work several hours by the time I woke up for school and he didn't get home until shortly before I was getting ready for bed. When he did eventually get home on an evening, he was exhausted, but worse than that, my mother would immediately set about informing him about all the naughty things I had done that day. Please don't misunderstand, I wasn't a tear away hooligan by any stretch of the imagination. My biggest crimes ranged from not eating my vegetables to spilling Coca-Cola on my mum's brand new cream carpet. Regardless of the nature and scale of the malfeasance, my mother's default response was to shout "Craig David Beck, you wait until your father comes home". Needless to say, as a result of this ritual chastisement I was never particularly thrilled to hear my father's van pull up on the driveway.

When I look back on my childhood I don't remember seeing much of my father and when I did, I recall that he seemed to be angry with me a lot of the time. My Granddad Jack was the primary male role model in my life. A giant of a man, who worked in the steel mills of Darlington, from the age of 14. To me, he was the strongest, funniest, most invincible man who ever walked the planet. I loved him dearly and he shaped me into who I am today. Most obvious is my sense of humor and appallingly uncool taste in music. I grew up sitting on my Granddad's knee watching wartime black and white comedies, by the likes of Will Hay, Arthur Askey and Abbott and Costello. While occasionally he would lift me onto his shoulders and carry me down to the local working men's club, where hard working, scary looking men from the steel foundry would sit drinking cheap beer, while listening to country and western music.

On a weekend, Jack would balance me on the cross bar of his bicycle and take me to his allotment where he would tend to his vegetables. He also kept a few chickens and pigs, which would terrify me most of the time. One memory that still lingers to this day, is the time he was trying to fix a broken fence and the tool he was working with slipped and sliced a gaping wound in his left forearm. Blood ran furiously down his arm from a nasty looking cut. I was frozen to the spot in total shock and horror. While Jack simply glanced at the wound and shook his head, like it was nothing more than a paper cut. He seemed more irritated by the inconvenience of it, rather than responding to the pain. This and many other events of my childhood, firmly positioned this man as an invincible God in my young life.

It is for this reason that I didn't display any emotion when my brother called to tell me he had died. It simply didn't make sense, he couldn't die, he was invincible. He had not been ill, and as I later found out, he had simply dropped down dead in front of the TV. He had reached for his giant cup of tea and something in his gut had gone bang and he died of an aneurism. No warning, no indication that the last time I saw him would really be the last time that I saw him.

A day before the funeral, I traveled up to my home town of Darlington from Preston, where I was working at a radio station called Rock FM. Still, I couldn't quite get my head around the idea that Jack was gone, it just didn't seem possible. I asked my mother for the address of the funeral parlor where his body was laying. I thought if I saw his body it might help me come to terms with his death. However, my mother thought this was a terrible idea and ever trying to protect me, she asked me not to go. She told me that he looked terrible and actually nothing like the man I remember. She suggested it would be better to leave my memories of him intact and think back to all those wonderful times of my childhood. I never did see his body, the coffin was carried into the crematorium and placed on a table, before two thick purple curtains closed slowly, as a hymn played on the speaker system. Then we all filed out of the room in tears and that was that. Death without ever really facing it!

When you play peek-a-boo with a baby, the reason it fascinates and entertains so effectively, is because the baby doesn't have a sufficiently developed brain to understand that just because he or she can't see you, it doesn't mean you have ceased to exist. From the baby's point of view, you are literally vanishing into thin air in front of his or her tiny confused face. In the West, we treat death in exactly the same way, we hope that if we can't see it then it doesn't exist. As though our attention to something gives it the power to exist and if we don't look, then perhaps we can make it disappear.

This amazing man was there one minute and then gone the next. I don't really know what happened in between, something must have occurred, but I wasn't allowed to see it. I didn't really feel I was going through a process of grieving, but rather burying the whole event deep in my subconscious, rather than dealing with the reality of what had happened. People don't die in the West, they pass away, they lose their fight against their illness or they succumb to their injuries, but under no circumstances must they be allowed to die!

Chapter Two – 4th September 2015 Kathmandu, Nepal

"The fear of death follows from the fear of life. A man who lives fully is prepared to die at any time." Mark Twain

Kathmandu airport is not an airport by any such standard that I have ever experienced before, or since. When I landed in Kathmandu, I had to assume the pilot must have surely made some sort of grievous, navigational error. The fool seemed to have landed this Airbus A330 on a farmer's field, complete with a cow shed at the end of it. There was no way this could be Nepal's main international airport! Unfortunately, nobody else seemed shocked at where we had ended up and fellow passengers around me began the usual scramble to recover hand luggage from the overhead bins. A set of rickety steps was pushed up to the side of the aircraft and as I stepped off the plane and looked out into the Nepalese night, my only words were "oh shit"!

I had decided to visit Nepal with the intention of being a bit of a hippy and spending some time with the Buddhist monks in a monastery, buried deep into the Kathmandu countryside, a few hours drive from the capital center. When I booked this trip, I sat in my air-conditioned home office in my orthopedic, leather-backed recliner, with my MacBook on my lap. I sipped gently from an iced coffee and planned my spiritual adventure in Nepal. It all seemed so lovely and beautiful, I even dragged my partner to the cinema to see the new movie 'Everest' and wowed at the stunning scenery I was all set to experience with my own senses. I can only tell you that the reality of landing in Nepal to a pampered western author, such as myself, was the scariest experience of my life. Sadly, it only remained so for about an hour or so. That title would be trumped and claimed by the insane taxi driver who drove me at speed through the pitch-black streets of Kathmandu, in a car older than me. I never thought that you could nearly die that many times on such a short journey.

Eventually, I got to my hotel and locked myself in my room with the air conditioning cranked up high. I decided to leave the unpacking for another time and headed straight for bed, where I rocked myself to sleep, all the time reassuring myself that everything always looks better in the daylight. I told myself that Kathmandu will look a whole lot better after a good night's sleep and with a decent breakfast inside me. Needless to say, it didn't! I took a morning stroll through a district of the city, called simply 'Buddha', during the thirty-minute walk to an ATM that wouldn't give me any money, I must have stepped over twenty stray dogs - I still don't know if they were alive or dead. I dodged a goat that didn't like the look of me and avoided a cow that wanted to park a shit on my Nike's and all this is, before the monkeys that were swinging off the deadly looking mass of power cables lining every street, tried to steal my wallet. I was offered drugs, sex and some guy asked me to come home with him, so I could meet his sister and then marry her and take her to England with me. I politely declined and he assured me that she is very young and good at cleaning! Where the hell had I landed, perhaps hell itself?

After a few days of being constantly terrified, I started to relax a little. I decided it was time to experience some of the spiritual wealth of this third world country. While wandering around the tourist area and looking very much like a lost, confused tourist, I met a very friendly guy called Christian, who said that despite the fuel crisis that was in process, he had a car and petrol to show me around the temples and sacred areas of the city. He told me that I should come with him to his office so we could make plans for the following day. He proceeded to lead me down a dark alley, while I busily imagined as many possible ways I was going to be murdered. Eventually, once deep inside this rabbit warren, we arrived at a tiny office. Inside there was a mahogany desk, strewn with paperwork and maps and two metal folding chairs either side.

"So Mr. Craig, tomorrow I will have my best driver come and collect you", Christian said with a huge smile. The sort of smile that said 'ooooh I caught me a big fish here'. "Sounds good to me", I replied trying my best to look cool and collected like James Bond, but no doubt failing miserably.

"Good, good so that will be 8000 rupee Mr. Craig. Unless of course you want a bodyguard?", he said replacing the big friendly smile with an expression of concern. Or perhaps he was just skillfully mirroring my own facial expression. "Erm, do I need a bodyguard?", I asked with all the stupidity of a gullible tourist. You won't be surprised to hear that my good friend Christian advised to pay the extra amount and have a bodyguard accompany me on my exploration.

The next morning as promised, a car pulled up outside my hotel. Inside, I found a driver who didn't speak any English and a small child, who I eventually figured out was the bodyguard I had paid for! I am not sure what this boy was going to do if it all kicked off or I was attacked, perhaps cry for his mother and then she would come and save us both. Regardless of feeling a bit ripped off, we set off through the craziness of Kathmandu traffic. The driver skillfully weaving in and out of the livestock, dodging the beggars lying in the road and avoiding the worst of the potholes. Eventually we arrived at a huge temple on the banks of a river. The sun was out and there were hundreds of people sitting on the floor in little groups. Some were praying, some meditating, some cooking on little open fires and eating. It was peaceful and beautiful and so I decided to sit a while and watch the rituals of the locals who came to this holy place in their masses. I told my bodyguard that he could go back to the car and play with his Lego™ for a little while and I would call him if I needed any ninja protection!

After twenty minutes, I watched in confusion as an ambulance pulled up to the waters edge on the opposite side of the river. Two paramedics climbed out of the front and opened the rear doors, where they slid out a stretcher complete with a patient firmly strapped down. They carried the man or woman (I couldn't tell from where I was sitting) and lay them down by the edge of the water. Then blow me if they didn't just get back in the ambulance and drive away. I simply couldn't understand why they would just leave this person on the floor and what was even more strange, was that I was the only person who appeared to be paying the slightest bit of notice to the poor neglected soul. Shortly the penny dropped and I realized that this was a dead body. Someone who had either died in hospital that morning, or perhaps even in the back of the ambulance on the way there. I sat in silence staring at this dead body lying on the floor. For almost an hour, not a single person even looked twice. Countless people walked passed it and there were hundreds with a better vantage point than me, but nobody seemed in the slightest bit phased. I almost wondered if I was the only person who could see it.

But then the fairytale illusion was shattered, when several cars pulled up and half a dozen men and women got out. They surrounded the body and began to paint various parts of it with brightly colored red and yellow paint. When they were finished decorating the body of their loved one, the men of the family lifted the body off the stretcher and carried it over to a pre-prepared pile of wood. The pyre looked like it was constructed from six or seven wooden railway sleepers, stacked crisscrossed over the top of each other. They carefully laid their relative on the wood and then set it on fire. The family stayed until the body had burnt down to nothing but ash and then they proceeded to dispose of the remains into the slowly flowing river. The same river in which children were playing, just ten feet further down stream.

As crazy and barbaric as it all sounds to our coddled western senses, I began to wonder if actually it is us that have this death thing all wrong. We hide it away and wrap the event of dying in divertive language. We sanitize it, for God forbid that we have to think about our own death or the demise of those that we love. Forget the adults, here in this river, small children no older than four or five have just watched a dead body burn and they play on in the water where the remains are dumped, without pausing to take a breath. Little children entirely un-phased by death, while a forty-year-old western man sits on the opposite river bank with his jaw hanging open in shock.

"Now there really isn't anything radically wrong with being sick or with dying. Who said you're supposed to survive? Who gave you the idea that it's a gas to go on and on and on?

And we can't say that it's a good thing for everything to go on living. In very simple demonstration that if we enable everybody to go on living, we overcrowd ourselves and we're like an un-pruned tree.
And, so therefore, one person who dies in a way is honorable because he's making room for others… Although each one of us, individually, will naturally appreciate it when anybody saves our life, if we apply that case all around we can see that it's not workable.

We can also look further into and see that if our death could be indefinitely postponed, we would not actually go on postponing it indefinitely because after a certain point we would realize that isn't the way in which we wanted to survive.

Why else would we have children? Because children arrange for us to survive in another way by, as it were, passing on a torch so that you don't have to carry it all the time. There comes a point where you can give it up and say now you work.

It's a far more amusing arrangement for nature to continue the process of life through different individuals then it is always with the same individual, because as each new individual approaches life is renewed. And one remembers how fascinating the most ordinary everyday things are to a child, because they see them all as marvelous – because they see them all in a way that is not related to survival and profit.

When we get to thinking of everything in terms of survival and profit value, as we do, then the shapes of scratches on the floor cease to have magic. And most things, in fact, cease to have magic.

So therefore, in the course of nature, once we have ceased to see magic in the world anymore, were no longer fulfilling nature's game being aware of it. There's no point in it any longer. And so we die. And, so something else comes to birth, which gets an entirely new view. And so nature's self-awareness is a game worth the candle.

It is not, therefore, natural for us to wish to prolong life indefinitely. But we live in a culture where it has been rubbed into us in every conceivable way that to die is a terrible thing. And that is a tremendous disease from which our culture, in particular, suffers.

And we notice it personally in the way in which death is swept under the carpet. And, so a person is left to die alone, suddenly, unprepared, and doped up to the point where death hardly happens", Alan Watts

Have you ever sometimes felt envious of animals? Do you ever look at your cat sleeping peacefully by the fire and think 'you lucky bastard'?

While animals suffer a great deal and often die with little dignity, they deal with it all so much better than we humans do. For animals have the gift of being present, living moment by moment. At home we have two dogs called Contessa and Laika. We rescued them both from fairly appalling situations. It doesn't matter whether it's raining, blowing a gale or beautiful sunshine, when I come downstairs on a morning, they are both ecstatic to see me. Their eyes sparkling, they wag their tails with such enthusiasm that their whole body wiggles in a delightful expression of pure joy. I don't ever come down and find them looking depressed because they are worried about something. They never fail to get excited because they are scared that tomorrow I won't feed them, or that someone will steal their bed! In the precise moment that I walk down the stairs, they are happy; this is all they consider. This is a beautiful, peaceful place to be, something that most of us will never really be able to appreciate. Can you imagine what it would feel like to never worry about getting sick, whether you will be able to afford to pay the bills this month and ultimately to never fret over the knowledge that one day you will cease to exist.

I will be very honest with you; this book was never intended to be about our fear of death. I went to Nepal to have a spiritual epiphany, almost like I was demanding that the universe give it to me. This book was supposed to be about what I experienced in Kathmandu with the Buddhist monks I met. Without being aware of it I was trying once again to control the flow of life, trying to swim up the stream to get to a location I believed I needed to be. Rather than practicing what I preach and let go, allowing the water to take me where it wants to go.

Control, this is what we are all guilty of and it is the cause of all of our fears, misery and torment. The universe is a river, it knows exactly where it is going and it will not yield to our opinions. If we jump in the river and try and push the water back up stream, it simply ignores us and skirts around us, while we tire ourselves trying to achieve the impossible. Even though the force of the water may push us over and drag us backwards. The river is not angry at our intervention, it's just doing what it wants to do and allowing us to do what we want to do too.

Of course we are not always fighting against the flow, because in good times we quite like the direction the river is taking us. However, then we fail to enjoy what is happening because we get attached to it and become afraid that the direction will change from something we like, to something we do not like. In our anxiety, we miss the beauty of the moment while we are busy trying to freeze the river where it is. Can you see that if you did succeed in what you were fighting so hard to achieve and actually freeze the river in place, then it instantly ceases to be a river at all. You got want you wanted but you lost everything in the process. We create misery in our lives by constantly creating these loops. Constantly creating situations where we believe that we need something to make us happy, but then when we get what we want, it ultimately makes us miserable.

This is true of everything in life, even death. If I performed a magic spell and told you that you are now immortal, you will never die. Would that make you happy? Probably, well at least for a little while, but how long would it be before you tired of being alive and wanted to stop? Can you see that even if you get this definitive prize of never having to die, the very thing you said you needed to be happy, will still ultimately make you miserable.

The direction and purpose of this book changed on 12th August 2016, and it was an animal that forced it to do so. In May this year we found two kittens abandoned in a shed in downtown Larnaca, Cyprus. We started taking food and water to them on a daily basis, until one day we went and found that there was only one kitten left. A little girl of about 4 weeks old, but her sibling had ventured across the road and now lay dead in the gutter. The surviving kitten was in a pretty bad state. One eye had closed due to an infection and she was covered in dirt, fleas and ticks. I knew instantly what was going to happen and sure enough Nicola gave me 'the look' and the next thing we knew, we were on route to Mixhalis Louka's veterinary practice in nearby Oroklini. We called her April and she became the newest member of our little zoo. She got better quickly and soon became a bag of energy that terrorized our other cats without mercy. They hated her with a passion but she didn't care. Her cheekiness and boundless energy soon made her a part of the family and we fell in love with little April.

On 12th August 2016 April died. Nicola came rushing into my office with April in her arms. "Call Mixhalis and tell him April has been attacked by a dog", she said through tears. We rushed her to the vet and despite him battling to save her life for three hours, she slipped into a coma and died from her injuries. If you are an animal lover, you will appreciate just how heart breaking it can be to lose a pet. I know several people who would shrug and say 'It's only a cat', but to us she was a part of our life and her death felt unfair and undeserved. Naturally, being an author of many books such as this, I accept the concept of birth and death, but what haunted me with the death of April was that her life was seemingly pointless. If the universe has a plan, if we are indeed a part of an intelligence beyond our awareness, then what was the point of bringing a life into the world, putting it in a situation that gave it virtually no chance of surviving. Only to defy the odds and be saved, given a chance to live and then months later to have that life snuffed out for no logical reason?

I have never claimed to be a guru or someone who is perfect. In truth, I am more cursed than most. I am a classic over-thinker, but I believe my calling in this life is to find answers and spread a message. When something happens that doesn't make sense, I must apply order to the chaos before I can rest. When April died and Nicola and I cried our eyes out holding onto each other, it made me realize that as a species, we have a big problem, a problem that is probably at the route of all our self-destructive patterns; we are terrified of death! This single subject is big enough to dramatically affect our entire life. It doesn't matter how rich you get; how much sex you are having or how many amazing vacations you take each year. If you are sticking your head in the sand to avoid what is eventually coming your way, then you cannot be totally happy. Unless you are comfortable with the end, then peace, purpose and happiness are always going to be held slightly outside your reach. But more than that, I don't mean pre-deciding what final act you will accept from the grim reaper. Everyone would probably be happy to hear they are going to live to 110 and die while having amazing sex with a supermodel. But what if death for you comes tomorrow – is that ok too?

The fact that you bought this book makes me assume that the answer is probably 'no, no it's not really Craig'.

That's okay, because I believe you will eventually get to that point. Perhaps as a result of this book or maybe over the years that follow. You are already joining an elite group by virtue of the purchase alone. The fact that you are ready to read a book about death shows that you are not prepared to be an ostrich any more, you want to find peace with what is coming. This is a noble pursuit and you can expect the rewards to be profound and dramatic.

Chapter Four – Where the Hell is God?

"Your time is limited, so don't waste it living someone else's life. Don't be trapped by dogma - which is living with the results of other people's thinking. Don't let the noise of other's opinions drown out your own inner voice. And most important, have the courage to follow your heart and intuition. They somehow already know what you truly want to become. Everything else is secondary."
Steve Jobs

There are 4200 recognized religions in the world. Many people believe all of them are fake and the remainder of people believe that 4199 of them are fake. All of these faiths preach peace and love as a core value and so it is difficult to understand why such violence, prejudice and hatred runs rampant, throughout society at the moment. It feels like 2016 has been a truly terrible year for this planet, with barely a few weeks passing without another diabolical atrocity being reported by the media. We have seen a homophobic gun-man massacre the customers of a nightclub in Orlando, a young, right-wing German man kill indiscriminately in a Munich shopping mall and an articulated wagon being deliberately driven through the crowds of happy, French citizens, celebrating bastille day. The list of murder and hatred goes on and on.

I believe the driving force behind me writing this book now, is the contrast of the world to my own personal life. We all have our ups and downs, even the Queen of England declared her own Annus Horribilus (horrible year), a few years back. 2010 was my own personal hell, a year that very nearly brought me to my knees. I won't expand on the events of that period in my life, because I think I have mentioned the nightmare of that year in prior books. Let me just summarize it for you by saying that if it could go wrong, it did go wrong for me in 2010. By contrast, today I am sitting writing this in the sunshine outside the Larnaca immigration office, while waiting for my appointment to formalize my residency here in beautiful, peaceful Cyprus. The last twelve months have brought me more peace, love and happiness than I have ever experienced before. Again I won't expand much further on that because let's face it, there is nothing more sick inducing than some old hippy banging on about how wonderful and beautiful his life is. I will summarize it briefly for you as such; I live in the sunshine with the woman of my dreams and my four happy rescue animals (the zoo). I love the people and animals with whom I share my life, with great passion and I feel loved back in equal measure. I don't go to work (haven't for many years) and there is nothing I want or need. My goal in telling you this and in deed my goal in writing this book is to share what I have discovered over the years, so that if you are not currently where you want to be in life, then you can bring about positive change and start to find your own peaceful path in this angry world we call home.

Just like jumping from the sauna into a freezing cold swimming pool. My own personal bliss only serves to highlight and amplify my perception of the misery and hatred bubbling under the surface around the western world. The terrorism we see almost continually on the rolling news channels is easy to point at and condemn, but there is something more powerfully dangerous than the actions of a few radicalized mad men. More potent, is the general mindset of the people, for when a whole nation feels hate and prejudice, the universe swings into action in a disastrous way. Take for example the horrors of World War II, it's too easy to point the finger of blame entirely at Adolf Hitler and say that the lone actions of an unstable narcissist were ultimately responsible for the deaths of millions of men, women and children. The reality we must accept, is that no one man can wield such power without the mindset of the people behind him. Hitler came to power because Germany had been totally humiliated by defeat in World War I. Europe and its allies set about punishing the German nation and saddled the country with so much debt that unless something had happened, they would have still been paying it off well into the late 1980's. Inflation ran rampant until the currency became so worthless, that people would literally carry all the money they needed to buy a loaf of bread to the baker in order to buy it.

The German population were on their knees, when along came a lunatic singing a song they could identify with.

Hitler raised a fist to the rest of the world and proclaimed that enough is enough, and the people cheered him on. We like to think that such a situation could not happen again, but I believe it is folly to rest easy with such an assumption. In the United Kingdom, we just witnessed a situation that isn't so far removed from the birth of Nazi Germany. The recent referendum which decided whether the United Kingdom should remain a part of the European Union, gave oxygen to some insanely right-wing personalities, who in any modern day society should not be permitted a moment's exposure to the masses. Under the battle cry of 'it's time to take back our country', opportunistic 'politicians' such as Nigel Farage encouraged people to vote against the migrants who had arrived in the UK over the past years. They used propaganda, fear and downright lies to convince a struggling population that the migrants were the source of all their problems and worries. The result was Polish and other eastern European children being bullied in school and told to go home. Synagogues and mosques were vandalized and covered in racist graffiti, and police forces across the country reported a 50% increase in hate crimes against migrants. The media reported story after story of Muslim women being attacked at random. Punched in the face, kicked, verbally abused or pushed to the ground by the hate filled xenophobes of England, who now believed they had a mandate to attack minorities because the referendum vote went in their favor.

Adolf Hitler referred to the Jews as animals, not worthy of human respect, parasites that should be eliminated. Jewish stores and businesses were attacked, vandalized and avoided. Jewish people were eventually ordered to wear the star of David on their sleeve at all times, so people could identify them easily. Here we are, seventy years later and Donald Trump is calling for Muslims to be denied entry into the United States and that the ones who are already there, should be ordered to wear badges to identify themselves as such. Are the people of America up in arms at such a horrific suggestion, or is there a worrying majority who actually appear to agree with what this venomous individual is saying?

The source of all this hatred is fear and frustration. We become obsessed with trying to protect ourselves and our children's future, and completely forget about the current moment. This panic over trying to make the future secure, stems entirely from our inbuilt and regularly nourished fear of what is going to happen when we die. We tend to think that if we can somehow control the near future, then we will surely be capable of enforcing our will in the long-term future too. Religion has always been used to control the masses, with promises of future rewards for good behavior. The problem of course, is that good and bad are always subjective labels. Religions tell their followers that there is only one true God and it is a sin to worship any other. This gives the gullible and angry souls of the world, a license to attack and hate anyone who doesn't conform to their own subjective view of what

God wants. The single biggest problem with religion is this; the moment any one of us attempts to describe God, whatever we are describing, instantly ceases to be anything that remotely resembles God. You can't point at one thing and say 'that is God', for to do so, is to entirely miss the point. God is not one thing, he is not a man, it is not a thing, God has no location or destination. God is everything! You trying to describe God, is God and even you observing yourself trying to describe God is God. When religion gets involved and tries to make the concept of God easy to understand, only then do we hit the real problems. God becomes a fixed proposition and starts to become a figment of people's imagination. Then people start to worship the figment, rather than the higher power it was designed to describe. Once you take a cup of water out of the ocean, it ceases to be the ocean and once you try to define God, it ceases to be God.

Look at what happens when our species tries to put God in a box. We end up with people hating each other almost apparently at random. If you are different and don't fit into the agreed upon description of God and what he wants, then you are vulnerable to condemnation, abuse and attack. Homosexuals and people of other faiths are subjected to horrendous hate-fueled attacks, purely because they fail to fit the image, that a group of people have all agreed upon. Terrorists go on violent killing campaigns, all in the name of the illusion that they have enthusiastically labeled God.

If I set up my own religion and declare that God is a tall man, with no body hair and a bone through his nose, some people will be entirely comfortable with that image and others will recoil in horror.

I want you to disregard any image you may have already created to represent God in your mind. To help you do that, I am going to ask you to consider one of the most extreme theories of who or what God is. I neither agree nor disagree with the conclusion I am about to describe, but I do find it fascinating to consider the sheer enormity of scale that the scenario suggests.

Start with the premise that our universe is virtually identical to the composition of an atom. The Sun is positioned at the center as its nucleolus and the planets rotate around it, just as electrons do in the smallest element known to man. How big is an atom? Well, if I tell you that in a single grain of sand, there are approximately 500 sextillion atoms, then it will give you an idea of how small a thing we are talking about. From our subjective point of view, being a tiny human being with an extremely large ego, we consider ourselves to be pretty damn important. We also look out at the night sky and declare that we live in a truly vast universe. But what if planet Earth, the Sun, Mars, Venus and the Milky Way, all just make us one single atom in the REAL universe?

Now consider that in the human body, atoms combine to create cells, the building blocks of life. These cells multiply to form human tissue and organs such as the liver and kidneys. Each cell in the body contains around one hundred trillion atoms and the average human is made up of around seventy trillion cells.

Consider the possibility that God is really a vast life form and everything we know and believe to be real, actually represents one trillionth of one cell in the body of this indescribably enormous life. Our entire universe could simply be just a single atom residing within the body of our deity. Stop reading and think about that concept, because it will blow your mind at the scale and possible size of God.

It's such a dramatic and ultimately improvable theory that it doesn't warrant a great deal of consideration, but it does serve to put your overactive ego back in its place. While at the same time answering some very profound questions:

Where is God?

If we accept for a moment that we are merely a microscopic particle of God's eternal body, the only logical answer to this question is; he is everywhere, you are always connected to him, and essentially you are God.

Did he really create everything?

This is like asking if you created your own liver. Of course the answer is yes, even if you didn't do it consciously. Under this infinite premise, God not only created everything, he is everything. You are not a separate entity from your liver; it is a part of you.

What is the purpose of life?

In this context, the reason we live is purely to give life to God. We exist so he can exist; it's only our ego that refuses to accept this as the sole point of life, insisting we are more important than we really are. In this theory it also confirms that God loves and cares about us, we are essentially a part of him and he cannot exist without us and vice versa. If God cares for us in the same way that we care for our own cells, you start to see a similar pattern and explanation for the suffering on earth. Every day millions of cells in our body expire, only to be instantly replaced by new ones. Do we mourn the loss of those dead cells? Do we get upset that some cells died too young or unfairly? No, of course not, we just let them do what they were designed to do. It is not unfeasible to see God's interaction with us in a similar way.

Could it be that God cares as much for us as we care for our own liver cells? Surely we should all care about our bodies, as they are the only home we will ever have. However, perhaps cells are too small for us to really worry about and so we drink, smoke and do all those other things that kill cells by the million. We do this without batting an eyelid, in the same way most people would happily swat a fly dead, but the same people are unlikely to pick up a shot gun and take down a dog. It would appear size does matter in certain circumstances!

Too much time spent pondering the infinite possibilities of whom or what God is, will eventually melt your brain. Your conscious mind or ego is desperate to apply an answer to the question, but sadly it is not as powerful as it would have you believe. It is actually more of a curse than a blessing, as it is constantly over-emphasizing your importance in the grand scheme of things. Always suggesting in a very compelling way, that you are the most significant object in the world. Stephen Hawking's view on this, is that we are far too big for our boots and we are really nothing more than a very advanced and developed form of primate, nothing more. Some people will be offended by that statement and others will be scared by it. Sadly, all too many treat animals badly as though they are an entirely unworthy sub-species. It is ludicrous to these people to even suggest that cats and dogs might also go to heaven. So to insinuate, we ourselves are nothing more than advanced monkeys, ergo, it must also mean that we too cannot get to heaven.

Perhaps Stephen Hawking is correct and we are just primates with laptops and iPhones. So what if we are? This is only really a problem if you consider yourself more important than other members of the animal kingdom. The reality is, you are no more important than a dog, a cat or even the spider you accidently stood on the other day. If that suggestion depresses you, then don't allow it to, because the spider you crushed was God, the dog you rescued from the pound is God and the steak you had for dinner last night was God. So rather than feel depressed, instead, be pretty bloody humble and proud to be equal to the animals that surround you. God is not out there somewhere; we ARE God, the power to manifest a joyful life already exists within us. For all these years we have been searching for a treasure map, trying to find the location of the big Red Cross that marks the spot and all this time, we were standing on top of it.

Do you see animals rushing around to fit as much into their day as possible? Do you see animals in the wild suffering with stress and anxiety, because the field they live in is a mess or they are running short on their food collection targets this month? Of course not, and I will tell you from experience, that given a choice, cats will spend the vast majority of their day doing absolutely nothing at all, snoozing their life away. Our two cats, Mishu and Junior are lucky to have the comfort of a loving home and also acres and acres of land to explore and play in if they so wish. With all this adventure just a few steps away, they still choose a daylong snooze every time. You see animals are not terrified of one day dying and as such, they don't feel compelled to squeeze as much stuff into each waking moment for fear that, God forbid, we miss a single moment of pleasure that was due us!

In order to achieve peace in life, you have to embrace the temporary and stop trying to apply permanency to everything. The secret is to know that there has never been a storm that did not eventually end, but equally the heat wave also gives way when the time is right. Both good times and bad times will end and you have to accept that this is something that will never change. There will be times in your life when you are wealthy and you will experience times of wanting more. You will have good health and poor, but avoid the temptation to declare one of these to be good and the other bad. Neither label is appropriate, accept the ebb and flow of life, always expect things to improve soon.

You cannot fully embrace this principle until you deal with the biggest permanency of all, the event that the ego fears more than any other, death! You will struggle to be comfortable with the 'now' if you are terrified of the oblivion you believe is imminent. You need an exit strategy from this life, which means you need to be relatively clear in your own mind as to what is going to happen when you die. It doesn't really matter what you believe, as long as you believe something. So if you are an atheist and you believe when you die, that's it! Then that's fine, but you have to work on yourself so you can become comfortable with this. If you are worried about falling asleep one day and never waking up again, you are going to struggle to find peace in this lifetime. If at the moment you believe death means an eternity of oblivion, then you are experiencing fear and fear is always a sign that you are 'kicking'. If you are scared of what being dead feels like, let me ask you this…

Do you remember what it felt like before you were born?

Does that lack of knowledge upset or scare you?

If not, then what are you worried about? You have already been to the place you fear the most and it was fine, was it not?

If you are religious and you believe you are destined for heaven, then embrace that and take comfort in your belief. Really, it doesn't matter if you are right or wrong because either way, the belief will give you peace in this lifetime, in this moment and that is the only time that will ever exist. I respect your exit strategy, whatever shape it takes and I don't need you to have the same one as me or anyone else – there are no rules. As long as what you believe feels like it is based in love (and not kicking and screaming into oblivion), then you have an exit strategy that works. I will share with you what makes sense to me, my hope is that it resonates with you at a deep level and it adds to your sense of peace.

Firstly and most importantly, there is no such thing as death. You are not really you in the way that you currently believe; this is just the illusion of separation that we talked about earlier. There are not seven billion people on this planet; there is one person in seven billion containers. We place a great deal of focus on our birth and death, but only because this is the point where the ego became alive and is the point where that piece of meat in your head will die. From the point of view of who you really are, birth and death are largely irrelevant acts. It would be the same as drawing a cup of water from the ocean and declaring that in doing so, the water had now been born. Then, when you tip the cup back into the sea, the water has died (because it is no longer in the cup). When you look at it from this point of view, you realize that birth and death are also a profound illusion. The water existed before it was 'born' and it did not cease to be, after you emptied it from the container. If you can embrace the concept, that we are just one entity choosing to divide ourselves into billions of individual fragments and that in doing so, we accelerate our vibration and never ending expansion. It is then, that you will understand that you are not 'you' and I am not 'me' and as such, you cannot die because you also exist in me and in every living thing on earth. The day you die, you will be replaced by nearly 400,000 new lives. Everyday over 370,000 babies are born into this world, hundreds of thousands of new cups of water drawn out of the ocean and labeled as 'a new life'.

In short, you cannot die. Today, hundreds of thousands of new lives started and you are in every single one of them. Right now in this very moment, you are being cradled in the arms of your mother in Nigeria, you are being rushed into surgery in New York, you are meeting your grandparents for the first time in London, you are hearing the voice of your father as he holds his pride and joy in Berlin. Once you start seeing everyone as you, then all negative emotion (kicking up stream) becomes pointless. I understand this is a difficult concept to wrap your head around, but at the moment, the human race is like the branches of a tree, all living under the illusion that they are separate and different from all the other branches, just because at first glance that appears to be the case. If everyone is you, then why would you ever be jealous of your colleague who was promoted ahead of you at work? What would be the point in getting angry with the driver who cut you off on the highway and wouldn't murder, rape and other abuse be the most ridiculous thing you could ever do?

It took me a long time for this penny to drop; if I am being honest, it was probably a decade before it started to feel logical. Once the thought becomes a belief, then your life really starts to change. When you see the homeless guy begging for something to eat, he is no longer a stranger, instead he appears to be just another version of you, but one that has fallen on hard times. When you hear about children starving in Africa, the way you feel about it changes and it becomes more personal. You desperately want to help, to do something to ease their suffering. Can we agree that if everyone treated each other as though they were dealing with themselves, that the world would be not just better, but heavenly?

This is not a new concept that I have just invented, the theory that we are all the same, divine being has been around for as long as time itself. Eastern philosophy dating back thousands of years, makes constant reference to this idea and despite the countless wars and acts of terrorism that have been committed in the name of traditional religion, there is a *Golden Rule* in virtually every religious scripture you can think of.

"You shall love your neighbour as yourself. There is no other commandment greater than this." Mark 12:31 – The Golden Rule of Christianity

"Hurt not others in ways that you yourself would find hurtful" The Golden Rule of Buddhism

"This is the sum of duty; do naught onto others what you would not have them do unto you." - The Golden Rule of Hinduism

"No one of you is a believer until he desires for his brother that which he desires for himself."- The Golden Rule of Islam

"What is hateful to you, do not do to your fellowman. This is the entire Law; all the rest is commentary."- The Golden Rule of Judaism

"Regard your neighbour's gain as your gain, and your neighbour's loss as your own loss"- The Golden Rule of Taoism

The fact that this one simple belief is universally shared, I find breathtakingly beautiful and reassuring. Death is nothing to be afraid of and we have this all the wrong way around. Death is not the worst thing that will ever happen to us, it is the best thing. It is the one moment in life that forces us to exist in the now. The moment you die is the moment you die, there is no future to think about and the past is irrelevant. This is the single moment that we will finally experience life as we have been designed to.

It is precisely our instances on living outside of the current moment, that causes all our fear of loss and ultimately death. Right now as you are reading this book, death may feel like a pretty unpleasant experience. When you are young, fit and healthy, death is not something you can ever imagine wanting to happen. However, when your body is worn out and is causing you pain and misery, it is at this point you may welcome, even look forward to death. This applies to everything that we take out of the context of the now. If you eat until you feel sick, then you may feel violently ill at the thought of eating another meal. But if you don't eat for the next three days, then that same meal may become like heaven to you. If I tell you to go to sleep when you are not tired, you don't want to do it. However, if you are exhausted, then you gladly do as I request without objection. Our fear of death is caused by assuming that in the future, we will feel the same about it as we do right now. As we are not actually dying right now, there is no point predicting that we will not want it!

Chapter Five – A Question of Balance

"It is said that your life flashes before your eyes just before you die. That is true, it's called Life." Terry Pratchett, *The Last Continent*

Why do we have to die? The simple answer is because we get to live. Immortality would render life meaningless, there would be no context to give it a point. Think about it, there wouldn't even be a point to the word 'alive' if there was nothing else but 'alive'. The universe is in perfect balance, and this equilibrium is maintained without exception. The more we open ourselves up to pleasure, the more our capacity to suffer expands in equal measure. Or putting it in rather simpler terms, the higher we climb, the further we have to fall. This universal law is why people limit their potential so much, only the very few live an extraordinary life and it is the unspoken fear of death that keeps us restricted. For if you spend your time trying to avoid death, you will also end up avoiding life.

Not everyone attempts to deny death of course. Many people attempt to defy it by leaping from planes and climbing mountains. Of course it provides a distraction, but in reality it is just another way of avoiding accepting the end that will surely follow, and perhaps a lot quicker than it should if they keep jumping out of perfectly operational aircraft.

For the majority of society, the fear of dying is not a conscious thing. It is a fear buried deep at the heart of their subconscious and it presents itself by creating a scarcity mindset. The vast majority of people get stuck doing a job they don't love, living for the weekend or their next vacation. Life becomes about these brief moments of extravagance and not about the day to day. Unless you make peace with the concept of death, then to a lesser or greater extent, there will always be an underlying concern that life is pointless. With this at the back of their minds, people believe that happiness comes from external things, such as getting a new car or going on an expensive vacation. Happiness, peace and purpose become not only an external destination, but something in the future to aim for. We get so distracted by what we think we need to be happy that we miss the moment in which we are actually living and in desperation to get to that future destination, we sell the one thing we can't afford to lose: our time. We trade our time for dollars so that we may save up cash to buy the things and experiences that will ultimately fail to placate our anxiety. They can't do anything but fail because they are merely deflections from the true concern.

You cannot have life unless you accept that with it, comes death. This is how the whole universe is balanced and there is nothing that escapes this rule. Without loneliness, hate and hostility we could not appreciate or give context to love. We want world peace, but it is impossible to find this utopia because it is a scenario that is out of balance. What we still have not understood as a species, is the harder we try to force our will on the universe, the harder it will push back to maintain the equilibrium. Take for example 'the war on terror', has it succeeded in destroying terrorism or does it appear to be getting worse? Of course it will get worse. The western world seems to be continuously hitting a revolving door, harder and harder and then getting angrier and angrier, because we keep getting hit in the back of the head!

Of course you may think this theory sounds familiar. This balance is often referred to as karma, but beyond Buddhist circles you are more likely to see the concept of karma used as a threat. Certainly if you observe social media, you will notice that karma seems to be more about revenge than it is about balance. Someone will post a status complaining about being treated unjustly by another person and a well-meaning friend will chip in with a 'don't worry honey, karma's a bitch' comment. This is not how karma works. I think this entirely misses the point and implies that God, the universe or whatever you want to call it, is someone or something on a mission to avenge misbehavior on our behalf. As I mentioned before, the universe is a river and if you jump in and consequently get knocked over by the rapids, it is not that the river wanted to punish you, but rather the result of your actions in applying force against the water and pushing in an opposing direction to the flow.

You might be wondering if it is really true, that striving to create happiness will be automatically balanced with the potential for pain in an equal measure. Then, is it not better to do nothing and live with the hand that we are dealt? Don't you see that this conclusion brings us back to the whole point of the book, to the reason that people stick in miserable jobs, living hand to mouth for a lifetime. If you avoid dealing with life, then you will also avoid dealing with death. If you have a crappy job that you don't like, then how much of a loss would it be if you got fired? Providing you could quickly replace it with another crappy job then it would be no loss at all, correct? But if you landed the opportunity to have the career you dreamed of since being a child, and get paid for it, then losing that would be painful and difficult to accept, would it not? But hopefully you can see that sticking with the crappy job is not a route to happiness. It may protect you from an event that may or may not happen, but in the process of constructing a safety net against your anxieties becoming solid, you also make yourself miserable as a by-product.

I really want you to understand that I am not standing atop an ivory tower, dishing out this advice. I do not see our relationship as master and student. I believe we are kindred spirits making a journey together, learning and discovering together. I tell you honestly about my faults and past mistakes because I want you to know that you are not broken. Our struggle to understand the gift of life is commonly shared and what I have discovered, is the more intelligence you have, the harder your struggle will be. I have often joked how wonderfully peaceful it must be to be blissfully stupid, but of course I don't really aspire to achieve stupidity, that would be... stupid.

Chapter Six – 7th March 2016

"Because God is never cruel, there is a reason for all things. We must know the pain of loss; because if we never knew it, we would have no compassion for others, and we would become monsters of self-regard, creatures of unalloyed self-interest. The terrible pain of loss teaches humility to our prideful kind, has the power to soften uncaring hearts, to make a better person of a good one." Dean Koontz, The Darkest Evening of the Year

In the 1980's when my friend's father had a new computer installed at his business premises, we all gathered in the street to watch its arrival. Such was its size, the entire roof of the building had been removed to accommodate its installation. It arrived on the back of a flat bed truck and was hoisted into position with a crane that had also been hired at great expense to complete the delivery.

An entire office had been cleared and made available for it, and yet it was capable of no more than the basic functions of our modern day calculators. In the realm of information technology, we have progressed a long way in a short time, to the point that we now casually carry cell phones with ten thousand times the computing power than that Goliath of a machine had. You only need to look back at some of the predictions made for computers by the popular science magazines of the day, to realize just how much we have exceeded expectations.

The worldwide market was predicted at one point, to be just five machines, and another publication proudly declared that one day, all computers would weigh less than 1.5 tons! Today, the machines that our children use just to play computer games on, have infinitely more processing and memory than the machines that were used in the space technology that thrust the first man into outer space. However, while humankind can crow about its computerized revolution, we still have only created a device with less than 1% of the power of the human mind.

You can learn even the most complex of computer languages within five years, yet you can spend a lifetime not quite getting to grips with the possibilities of your own internal computer. Programmers spend years in training to diligently understand the power of their machine, before they start to generate code of any value. One of the first lessons they learn is through the acronym GIGO, which stands for Garbage In, Garbage Out. Sadly, most people don't apply the same discipline to programming their own internal computer, a machine with the power to create literally anything.

Everything that you believe is wrong with your life exists purely because of bad programming in your subconscious mind. If you are overweight and unhappy about the size or shape of your body, it is due to a subconscious level of belief that you actually want to be in that state. Many will object in the strongest terms to a statement like that, but you can't possibly know at a conscious level what is stored in your subconscious mind. It would be akin to claiming you can carry the world's oceans in an eggcup. For the moment, I ask you to suspend your disbelief and stick with me as I explain…

This principle applies to everything that you would describe as good and bad in your life. A dependence on alcohol and other drugs is the unconscious belief that those chemicals are the best way to deal with pain being generated by your conscious thoughts. The perception that being seen in an expensive and flashy looking sports car makes you look more important, is a scenario generated by your egoic mind and that has been repeated enough to become a subconscious belief. Perhaps from this point on, it may be better to refer to beliefs like this, as nothing more than a lie, the word 'believe' even has the word 'lie' in the middle of it as a reminder. When desires of the ego become so embedded in our image of ourselves, they become automatic or subconscious. This is dangerous and self destructive because of the power available to this part of you. The subconscious has a direct line to the divine power of the soul.

I feel an objection coming on! 'If the subconscious has the power of the soul, why doesn't it prevent the bad instructions from being completed? Why on earth would it sit back and allow a self-destructive program to run?' Good question, but who says it's a bad program? I admit that's a little flippant, and we can all come up with illusive responses to tricky questions – it's how psychics, mediums, politicians and other charlatans earn their daily bread. Let's deal in fact to fully understand how our brain operates. It is commonly accepted, that our mind is split into two unequal halves that allow us to experience life on contrasting levels; consciously with our thinking mind and unconsciously with the infinitely larger and more powerful part of our mind, we call the subconscious. Nothing portrays the delusion of power held by the conscious or egoic mind quite like the story of a little dog, named Biba.

Biba was the nasty little Jack Russell terrier my girlfriend had when I was 16 years old. This dog had a serious attitude problem; it was no bigger than a sofa cushion but had the aggression and belief that it was a fearsome Rottweiler. Every time I would visit my girlfriend, admittedly hoping for a bit of alone time with her, Biba would sit in the window, watching me walk up the path to the house. Before I even had the chance to knock on the door, it would launch its pathetic and laughable attack. Occasionally I would see a flash of it's little, white, needle-like teeth through the letterbox. Once inside, it would sit on my girlfriends lap snarling at me.

This 1 foot high, 10 pound deluded animal actually looked at me, a 6'1", 196lb man and thought "just let me at him and I will rip him to pieces". The reality as Biba often discovered, is that he was so small I could remove him from the room without even bending over. Simply by placing my shoe under his belly I could lift him and carry him out into the kitchen on the end of my foot, his legs kicking and teeth snapping all the way. With a grin across my face I would lock him in before sauntering back to my girlfriend, all the way listening to the furious muffled barking. For her sake I would agree with her that he was indeed a little cutie. I didn't believe that letting her know my true feelings for this repulsive little rat would have done me any favors.

Biba is how I see the conscious mind; it is a small, inefficient part of your mind that thinks it's much bigger and more important than it really is. It also has all the decorum and attitude of that little dog too. Your ego is the voice in your head that judges and questions everything in and around your life. As a child, as you stood on the starting line of the school race, the ego was there, whispering in your ear. What is whispered is unique to you and what your ego wanted at that moment (some believed they could win and they did, some believed they couldn't and they didn't).

The voice begins quiet and grows as strong as you will let it; ever present in all areas of your life, at home, work and even socially. When you walk into a bar as a singleton, it is the voice that tells you that you are more attractive and good looking than that person, but less so than another. As you watch a person drive past you in the car of your dreams, it is the voice that tells you how you should feel about that person's public display of success. It either views the scene as something that you should also have (in order to be happy) or as an example of your lack of self-worth.

Books such as Rhonda Byrne's 'The Secret', try to make you aware of this instinctive reaction of the ego, and instead of responding as the ego dictates, make positive statements of intent instead. It suggests that instead of envy, you see yourself sitting in that car and enjoy the positive image you have painted in your mind's eyes. This is laudable and certainly better than any negative emotion, but again if it is purely willpower arguing with the ego, it is largely pointless. It is for this reason that so many try the techniques described in 'The Secret' and other 'power of attraction' books, but give up when they see little evidence of success. Only the subconscious can create, in spite of the continuous diatribe coming from the ego. In short, you can say anything you want about yourself, it doesn't make the slightest bit of difference to what you can achieve. I can wake up every morning, stand in front of the bathroom mirror and with all the confidence and positive mental attitude I can muster, state that I am a professional football player. Unless I subconsciously believe that ridiculous scenario is even possible, then the chance of it becoming reality are somewhere between slim and none.

On one side of the coin, this appears frustrating that we can't manifest our desires so easily, but on the other side and with some knowledge of the perfectly horrendous scenarios our thinking mind can create, it's probably for the best. Have you ever stood on top of a tall building and wondered just for the briefest of moments, what it would feel like if you fell? Do you still want to give the conscious mind the power to create our dreams?

We all allow the ego to become so vocal that we begin to believe that it is who we are; we actually become the voice in our head. This is ultimately the source of all unhappiness and discontentment in life, the ultimate illusionist responsible for all the pain, but a master at laying the blame elsewhere. All input from this voice is generated by the need to avoid fear. With that in mind, it's not difficult to see why egoic dreams and indeed any desire born of a negative emotion, is unlikely to be beneficial in the long-run. The conscious mind simply can't stop judging and answering questions, even if it doesn't know the answer. Such is the predictability of the ego, that I can demonstrate its weakness with a few statements and questions that I would like you to try NOT to answer.

"What is 2+2?"
"What color are your eyes?"

"What ever you do, don't think of an elephant!"

Like a puppy chasing a ball, your conscious cannot help itself; it simply must answer all questions asked of it. This isn't entirely a problem, as without this feature of the human mind, you would be dead by now. Whilst your conscious mind comes up with some pretty ill-advised opinions about you and what you need to be happy, it also does a job of protecting you by judging all the situations you find yourself in on a daily basis. As you stand on the side of a busy road waiting to cross, your conscious mind evaluates the speed and distance of approaching traffic and decides at what point it is safe for you to cross the road. The reason why young people and the elderly are more at risk of injury in these situations is further evidence of the weakness of the ego.

Children do not have enough information to accurately judge the risk and the elderly are using outdated perceptions. The conscious uses what it believes to be true to make the judgment. No doubt at some point when you were a child, you picked up a hot pan on the stove and discovered quite quickly how much a burn can hurt. The lack of knowledge meant your conscious was incapable of judging the situation as a threat, but from that point on you will be much more cautious in the same environment. Taking this into consideration, you may now feel some gratitude towards your ego for acting so effectively at these points and saving you from serious harm. However, you should also be able to see that all these heroic acts are all motivated by nothing positive, but rather the simple desire to avoid pain/fear. The ego has no regard for your best interests; it only cares about what it wants. It is unwise to mistake its protection for care.

Sometimes the by-product of what the ego desires coincidently serves your 'wellbeing' at the same time, but it is not there by design, you just got lucky on that occasion. The ego is quite willing to cause you immense suffering, purely to get to the outcome it desires. Should the ego desire a specific material possession (or rather the feelings generated by attainment), it will apply significant pressure in the form of emotional pain until you give it what it wants. Then of course, as soon as you comply, it rewards you briefly before beginning the process over again, with even more intensity. This book is taking you on a journey of awareness and part of that is developing the ability to observe the ego as a third person trying to manipulate you, rather than believe that you and your ego are one and the same.

If by this point you are not feeling too schizophrenic, let's talk about the larger and significantly more powerful subconscious. A polar opposite to the ego, the unconscious mind judges nothing; it is completely at peace and feels no need to compare you to others. It wants for nothing, needs nothing and fears nothing; operating in a divine state, existing purely in the moment. Nothing that has gone before is relevant and the future is considered equally unimportant. The only thing that has relevance is the now, and in each and every moment, your subconscious dutifully completes the programs that reside within itself with perfect accuracy. This is why you don't have to consciously beat your heart, control your body temperature or any of the other millions of functions happening in your body, every second of every day.

During the time it has taken for you to read that last sentence your subconscious has destroyed and replaced 50,000,000 cells in your body. Its power is simply awe-inspiring. Ridiculously sitting at the feet of this awesome power, and like Biba the bad attitude dog, is your conscious mind and it actually believes it is equal to, if not more powerful than your subconscious.

This is the very embodiment of arrogance and pomposity; it's like a three legged, blind donkey, insisting it could take on and beat a multimillion-dollar racehorse. If suddenly your ego became responsible for everything that is currently looked after by the subconscious, you would be dead in less than a second.

But you may be wondering why your ego is such an utter douchebag? The answer is simply this; the ego is acutely aware of its temporary status. It knows (as much as it tries not to think about it) that it is nothing but a piece of meat inside your head. It's a physical construct of your earthly body and nothing more. Most people think they are body that has a soul; this is the wrong way around.

We are souls who have a body. The way most people think is a bit like believing that when you get inside a car, you become the car itself. Now imagine that once inside the automobile, the car started to act like it was you, making demands and insisting that you go where it wants to go. This is what your ego is doing all the time, it is under the delusion that it is who you are. The ego is nothing more important to your eternal existence than your left leg is.

Deep down the ego knows that the end is coming, it knows that your body will eventually break down and you will get to the point where you no longer wish to remain in it. Life will become painful and infective and you will choose to die, leaving behind your ego and its insanity. This thought is terrifying to your ego and if you allow it to do so, it will spend an entire lifetime kicking and screaming, trying to prove that it can avoid death, fruitlessly trying to make your current body a permanent fixture.

The river of life is always moving and as soon as you observe the river, it has already ceased to be the thing you initially observed. You can't freeze it or reverse it and there is nothing you can do but observe it in the precise moment that it exists. For example, I may give you $50 and instruct you to go to the river and fill a bucket so that I might own my own piece of it. Upon your return, I would demand a refund because the bucket of stagnant water would not in any way resemble a river.

Permanency does not exist in any form in our world. Everything living, everything nature placed here and everything we build will eventually crumble and fall. Nothing is saved; death and destruction are like the outward breath of God. He breathes in and life is created, trees grown and buildings emerge. He breathes out and people die, trees burn to the ground and buildings collapse.

Sadam Hussain spent a lifetime building as many statues of his image as possible, he commissioned hundreds of portraits to be painted and even officially named Iraq's main airport, Sadam Hussain International Airport. He did all this in a vain attempt to live on after his death – he failed. Virtually all the statues were pulled down and the airport was renamed.

If you are pinning your happiness and success in life on achieving permanency, then you are destined to fail. At the end of your days, when you lay in your deathbed considering your vast property portfolio and the millions of dollars in the bank, you can be sure that you would happily trade it all for just one more week alive.

More subtly than that, we all also get attached to the idea of permanency when we give ourselves labels. Do you not think at some point when Adolf Hitler was growing up, his mother sat him on her knee and said 'Adolf you are such a good little boy'. Was she wrong, or perhaps she was right but only in that moment?

All too often we take these labels and decide that they are a permanent description of who we are.

- I am a good person (how do you know you always will be?)
- I am a fast sprinter (will that always be the case?)
- I have high standards; I will never stay in a hotel with less than a 5-star rating (Never?)

When I coach people one-to-one, they normally approach me with a label that they have decided is permanent. They come up to me and say 'I am a terrible public speaker, I always make a fool of myself' or 'I have terrible bad luck, nothing ever goes right for me'.

If you believe there is anything about your life that is permanent, then I want you to spend some time thinking about how that could possibly be true in a world where it's impossible. I apply this just as much to the good stuff as the things we call 'bad'. I would call myself a 'good parent'; I love my children deeply and without question. However, I am willing to admit that at times I have made mistakes, given bad advice, shouted when I should have hugged and generally been a 'bad' parent. Especially during the challenging teenage years where my kids were striving to break free and be individuals. So which am I? 'A bad parent' or 'a good parent'? In reality, no label serves any useful purpose beyond the moment it is expressed in.

Good times will end and life will blindside you with events that spoil the fun. In the dark times, the storm will come to an end and bright sunshine will once again fill your life. This is the ebb and flow of the universe – God will breathe in and God will breathe out.

Call this an exercise if you will, but I want you to examine your life for incidents of where you have tried to escape loss by avoiding life. Perhaps it will be the job you didn't go for incase you were rejected or an opportunity missed because you were afraid of risk.

I will help you do this exercise by critiquing my own life and showing you how you can take action to make dramatic and powerful shifts in your contentment, peace and purpose. Let me start by telling you that my parents have the traditional view of relationships. That being, that you meet a girl, go steady, get married, have kids and stay together forever – regardless of how happy you are. For that reason, they have long ago given up on trying to understand my lifestyle. It would be fair to assume that they think their son is a bit flimsy when it comes to relationships. It is true that I am guilty of previously being a serial monogamist, flowing from one short-term relationship to the next. If I tell you that I am 42 years old and I have never been dumped, you may first assume that I am boasting, but the truth is far from that. I ended all my past relationships because I never really committed myself 100%. In my own self analysis, it would be easy to stop at the conclusion that I am just another guy afraid of commitment, but I believe my eleven-year marriage and two happy kids suggest that it is a bit more complicated than that. You see, when you give your heart to someone else, you also give them the power to give you pain in equal proportion to the love you will accept. Going from one bad relationship to another is just the same as staying in a crappy job you do not like. Before I got to grips with my own relationship anxiety, I was desperately trying to keep one hand on my independence and on other such safety nets, while also trying to force a loving relationship into my life. If you are serious about this aspect of your life, then it is a bit like skydiving. You either do it or you don't! You can't keep one hand on the plane just in case, this very action may keep you safe but it also means you are not really skydiving. Unless you give the other person complete access to your heart, then you are not really in a complete, loving relationship.

Being conscious of the things in your life that are causing you misery is eighty percent of the battle to free yourself of their burden. You should take great pride in the fact that you are reading this book because this is a fear that most people would rather pretend they did not have. Personally, I knew I had some issues around relationship anxiety and I had to work on myself to let go of this bad program that was running in my subconscious. On 7th March 2016 a woman came into my life that changed everything. I will spare you the sickly stuff, but everything felt different and despite my usual confidence in dating situations (I have done a lot of it), I felt completely out of control this time. Rather than the usual excitement, lust and passion I would expect from the beginning of a relationship. You know, the stuff that lasts for a few weeks or months and then slowly fades away, until you eventually get to the point where you can't understand how you even had the energy to have sex three times a day! Well, this time it was different. Of course there was all that exciting stuff too but there was an overriding feeling of peace, a strange and unexplainable sensation that I was home at last. I very quickly (almost embarrassingly quickly) realized that Nicola was a woman I could (and would) fall deeply in love with. The problem was if I continued to do what I had always done in relationships, I was certain to get the same self-destructive outcome as before. After a few months, I would push her away to prove to myself that I don't need anybody but myself. I would make myself miserable while I was busy trying to protect myself from being miserable. I can't claim I made a conscious decision because everything that happened just kind of happened. But for the first time in my life, I cut all the safety nets, I gave her 100% of my heart and with it, I gave her the potential to cause me more pain than I feel I am built to cope with. However, I believe it is the balancing action of the universe that matches that potential to cause hurt, with the potential to love. I wanted love and peace in my life, but my focus was solely on not losing that once I eventually found it. My thoughts, words and deeds were all in a time that does not exist.

All things like this are little reflections of our ultimate fear. The day you give yourself permission to die, the perfect death is the day you give yourself permission to live the perfect life. Now it's your turn, take an honest look at your life and examine what things you do to protect yourself, that when you look at them with new eyes will appear to be nothing more than attempts to prevent misery, by making yourself miserable.

This is not the sort of thing you can do in ten minutes; it can take days or weeks, but give yourself permission to allow this thought to linger around at the back of your mind for as long as is needed. Then take action to embrace the things you are afraid of. If you're currently doing a job that you cannot be positive about, you just cannot bring yourself to think anything positive about it, get out of that job now. You will never become wealthy or rich in that job.

Did you know that eighty per cent of the world's workforce hates their job? In fact, 'hate' probably isn't a strong enough word, they DESPISE their job. They turn up, they put their head down and for eight hours they hate, hate, hate their job.

Negative, negative, negative flows through every fibre in their body. That means that people on average, everywhere, are spending about 40 hours every week doing something they hate and trying to get wealthy doing it. It's stupid, it will not work. It's time to wake up and smell the coffee... You can only be successful in life if you're doing what you enjoy.

Why's that so? Well it's because you're performing the work of your heart and soul - what you enjoy. You create a special vibration with your thoughts and your emotions. Your thoughts become positive automatically, you don't have to work at it. You're always a positive thinker when you're doing something you enjoy.

If you are currently doing a job you don't enjoy, that you're doing merely to pay the bills and keep the wolves from the door, you will not become rich. It's not the way to success. Your job or life's work should not be something you hate, especially when it takes up most of your energy, your creativity and your life.

It's my deepest desire that with the help of this audiobook you will discover for the first time in your life, what you really, honestly, truly want. That, coupled with the practical application of the skills in this series of books, will transform you into a shining beacon of happiness, peace and purpose.

Of course I don't know you personally, and the chances are good that we have never met. However, I believe that even without meeting you I already know two fundamental things about who you are, how you feel and what you really want to happen next. If you are anything like me, you will have always had a nagging sensation that you are here to do something important. You understand there is great potential inside you and life has an important mission for you. This sensation is what Nazi war camp survivor, Victor Frankl described as the existential vacuum. It is literally a black hole in your being that is created by the failure to follow your heart and complete the task that you are really here to do. This hole is painful and uncomfortable, it is always there at the background of your existence and it won't go away until you fill it back up.

My brother in law once set up a business called SAHAFI. I asked him what the company does and he replied 'anything'. Being rather confused by his answer I asked what the name meant and he revealed that it was an acronym for 'See A Hole And Fill It'. This is an instinctive response of human beings and we approach this internal vacuum with the same sticking plaster approach. We know there is a dull ache inside us, created by this emptiness and so we desperately try to fill it up. Our favorite ways to do this are with material possessions: sex, drugs and alcohol and all other things earthly and physical. This universally pursued attempt to fill the hole, is as effective as trying to fill a volcano by throwing matchsticks into it. Fruitless, pointless and a waste of time!

How many people do you know who give everything they have to climb the corporate ladder, to achieve the next pay scale, to get the car with upgraded leather interiors?

How many people do you know choose where they live or the car they drive by comparing it to what their friends and neighbors have?

How many people do you know who max out their credit card so they can have a television at least two inches bigger than their friends have?

Does it ever make any of them happy, I mean truly a genuine sensation of peace and contentment with life? Maybe for a few days, even possibly for a few weeks, but never (and I really do mean never) for a lifetime. Money, cars, boats, houses, vacations, gadgets, technology and all this other 'stuff' we dream of owning, are nothing more than matchsticks for the volcano. I don't know what your true purpose in life is, but I do know that it is not to own a great automobile or only ever stay in five star hotels. Stop avoiding life and do the thing you love. When the hole is filled, you are going to find that love, peace, happiness and joy flooding into your life. All the things that you thought would bring happiness, such as money, sex, vacations and abundance are not actually how you create happiness, they are the result of being happy. The entire western world has got the whole puzzle the wrong way around. When you fill the vacuum, then all the good stuff will automatically flow into your life.

"Whatever happens, they say afterwards, it must have been fate. People are always a little confused about this, as they are in the case of miracles. When someone is saved from certain death by a strange concatenation of circumstances, they say that's a miracle. But of course if someone is killed by a freak chain of events -- the oil spilled just there, the safety fence broken just there -- that must also be a miracle. Just because it's not nice doesn't mean it's not miraculous." Terry Pratchett, Interesting Times

If you ask most people what the opposite of life is, they will say it is death, but this is not correct. The opposite of death is birth and both events are entirely natural and joyful moments of life. Death is something to be celebrated because without it, nothing makes sense, nothing has depth or meaning. When we deny death, we are forced to live in a shallow world where the superficial and the external are desired and ruthlessly pursued. However, doesn't that exactly describe the mindset of the western world and most of its inhabitants? If you fully accept and embrace that one day you will die, then it naturally follows that you will also struggle to find value in having a car better than your neighbor. You will quickly realize that no matter what you do to make your life appear more significant than the next person, you will ultimately fail to win such a shallow victory.

Imagine if the temperature was always the same. Day in, day out, no matter where you were in the world, inside or outside, the temperature was always a constant 22 degrees Celsius (71 degrees Fahrenheit). If this were true, there would be no such thing as summer or winter. Without the contrast of one over another, there would be nothing for us to label. Oh and boy do we love to label things.

A few years ago, a photography client paid me in cash, virtually everyone pays electronically these days, so I was a little unprepared for the request. I stuffed the bundle of one hundred Euro notes into my pocket and headed home. I forgot about the money and took my dogs out for a walk in the Cypriot hills. When I got home from the five mile walk, I remembered the €500 and reached into my pocket to retrieve the notes. Yes, you guessed it, they were gone. They must have dropped out of my pocket at some point on the walk. The dogs were absolutely thrilled because we headed straight back out and did the whole walk over. The whole way I was scanning the ground for my bundle of notes. I never found it! Of course most people would label this a bad day, but imagine the sort of day the person who found it had… but wait, forget that! Imagine what an amazing day my dogs had. Going walkies is like crack cocaine to my dogs – that day they slept like babies, having had the most fun day of their lives! So who says it's a bad day? My ego and that's all.

Every time you expose your ego to a little death, it will label it bad because it doesn't want to be reminded that it has once again failed to make things permanent. Whenever anything comes to an end, you experience a little death and you feel a physical pain attached to the loss. Whether this be from getting fired from a job, a relationship ending or someone you love dying. All these events are painful because they remind the ego of what is coming and until you fully embrace the end, you will continue to suffer little deaths throughout your life. Once you become aware of how aggressively we avoid talking about death, then you will realize how big the problem has become. We don't even particularly like the finality of saying goodbye to people and languages have evolved to reflect this fear. The French say 'au revoir' and the Germans say 'auf wiedersehen', both roughly translated mean 'until we meet again'. Only the Spanish seem to embrace death with 'adios', which means, 'I send you to God'. Perhaps its no coincidence that it's the language of people who actually have a day dedicated to celebrating the dead.

So our collective western ego labels birth as good and death as bad. When a baby is born, out comes the champagne and fine cigars and we congratulate the parents on their happy news. When someone dies we commiserate and say how sorry we are for their loss. But this is all because we insist on seeing life and death as opposites. It took a soap opera actor to give me a new paradigm on death, back in 2007.

Back in the 90's there was a very popular Australian soap opera that was shown daily in the United Kingdom. For some reason this program was off the scale popular, so much so that each episode was played twice a day, once at lunchtime and again in the early evening. I don't think I knew anyone back then who didn't at least know what was going on in the storyline. Neighbours is perhaps one of the most successful Australian exports of all time, eventually being watched in over sixty different countries around the world. It is the same soap opera that launched the careers of Jason Donovan and Kylie Minogue. One of the best-loved characters in the show was a pompous but lovable soul called Harold Bishop. His character was generally kind hearted, but a little prudish and very religious. The actor Ian Smith played the role in the series for over twelve years, making him one of the longest serving characters on the show.

On 21st March 2007, I was serving my notice at a radio station in Hull, England called Viking FM. I had been the Programme Director for the past few years and had recently resigned, having been offered a position at a bigger radio station in the North East of the country. As my replacement had already been appointed, I was a little surplus to requirements in the building. Ian Smith was in the radio station for an interview, which went so well that it overran, causing him to miss his train. As I had time on my hands and a company car sitting in the lot, I offered to drive him to his next interview in York, no more than an hours drive north. During the journey, I found out that rather than being a deeply religious man like his character Harold Bishop, he was in fact an atheist. I asked him if he was comfortable with the concept of oblivion that obviously must come as part and parcel of being an atheist. His answer left me speechless and gave me cause to repeatedly come back to his words over the next few days.

"Do you remember what it felt like before you were born?", he asked with a quizzically raised eyebrow.

"No", I replied, interested to see where he was going with this.

"Tell me, how many nights have you lay awake at night upset because of how it felt before you were born or even just upset because you can't remember what it felt like", he asked.

"None", I was forced to admit. I could see where he was going and I was annoyed with myself for not having a smarter rebuttal.

"Well then, that's how I feel about death. It didn't bother me before I was born and it won't concern or upset me after I die", he said with a knowing smile.

It doesn't really matter whether you believe in God and life after death. By saying 'I will accept death as long as I am convinced it is not the end', it is still an act of avoidance. The objective is to be at peace with your exit strategy. To know that this life will at some point in the future come to an end, and that is not just okay, but it is as beautiful as the moment you were born. What I have observed is that dying seems to be a bit like leaping out of a plane for your first parachute jump. It's horrific and terrifying until you've done it and then all fear fades away and you want to do it again. Do a little research of your own and you will find countless stories of near death experiences. The common thread does seem to be that once someone goes through a NDE, they lose their fear of dying.

Perhaps the most famous reported case of a near death experience belongs to Anita Moorjani, an ethnic Indian woman from Hong Kong, who had end stage cancer (Hodgkin's Lymphoma) and was being cared for at home. However, on the morning of February 2 2006, she did not wake up. She had fallen into a coma. Doctors said she would not make it beyond the next 36 hours, since her organs were no longer functioning and her body had started to swell up, creating open skin lesions. In spite of this, Anita saw and heard the conversations between her husband and the doctors that were taking place outside her room, about 40 feet away down a hallway. She also saw her brother on a plane, having heard the news that she was dying, coming to see her. Both things were later confirmed.

Then she claims to have "crossed over to another dimension, where I was engulfed in a total feeling of love. I also experienced extreme clarity of why I had the cancer, why I had come into this life in the first place, what role everyone in my family played in my life in the grand scheme of things, and generally how life works. I realized what a gift life was, and that I was surrounded by loving spiritual beings, who were always around me even when I did not know it. I found out that my purpose now would be to live 'heaven on earth' using this new understanding, and also to share this knowledge with other people."

In her now famous book, "Dying to be me", Anita explains how she "had the choice of whether to come back into life, or go towards death. I became aware that if I chose life, my body would heal very quickly. I then started to understand how illnesses start on an energetic level before they become physical. I became aware that everything going on in our lives was dependent on this energy around us, created by us. Nothing was real – we created our surroundings, our conditions, etc. depending where this "energy" was at. If I chose life, the results would show that my organs were functioning normally. If I chose death, the results would show organ failure as the cause of death, due to cancer. I was able to change the outcome of the tests by my choice. I made my choice, and as I started to wake up (in a very confused state, as I could not at that time tell which side of the veil I was on), the doctors came rushing into the room with big smiles on their faces saying to my family 'Good news – we got the results and her organs are functioning – we can't believe it!'. After that, I began to recover rapidly."

Doctors were quite surprised and once Anita became stable, they started tracking down the lymph nodes they saw when she entered the hospital. Tests had shown swollen lymph nodes and tumors the size of lemons, extending from the base of her skull all the way to her lower abdomen, but doctors found none. They did a bone marrow biopsy, again to find the cancer activity so they could adjust the chemotherapy according to the disease, but there wasn't any in the bone marrow. Because they were unable to understand what was going on, they made her undergo test after test, all of which Anita passed easily. She then had a full body scan, and because they could not find anything, they made the radiologist repeat it again.

"Because of my experience, I am now sharing with everyone I know that miracles are possible in your life every day. After what I have seen, I realize that absolutely anything is possible, and that we did not come here to suffer. Life is supposed to be great, and we are very, very loved. The way I look at life has changed dramatically, and I am so glad to have been given a second chance to experience 'heaven on earth."

Another story covered by the Daily Mail newspaper involved the near death of a pregnant mother of three, her name was Amanda Cable. The most significant aspect of Amanda's story is she concluded that dying actually taught her how to live.

One morning, I developed a nagging pain in my side. Within a few hours, it was so bad that I had to go bed. The rest of the family had been suffering from a stomach bug, and I just assumed I had caught it, too.
But two days later the pain was still there. I was in agony, unable to eat or walk. For the first time ever, I rang my wonderful GP and asked for an urgent home visit. I owe my life to the fact that he came to the house almost immediately, letting himself in with the spare key under the doormat.
My husband Ray was at work, and Ruby and her brothers — two-year-old twins Charlie and Archie — were enjoying the last day of their summer holiday at a playcamp.

Within five minutes of the GP's arrival, he called for an ambulance, and I was swiftly taken to the local hospital's A&E department. When I arrived, doctors discovered that I was pregnant. The baby was ectopic, meaning it had developed inside the fallopian tube instead of the womb. Ray was called at work, and he raced to be by my bedside.

Sadly, the quality of care I received was far from perfect. I was given morphine for the pain and sent to an upstairs ward for the night, despite tests revealing I had already lost a lot of blood from internal hemorrhaging.

I was also very upset that I would be missing Ruby's big day. I sent Ray home, begging him to get her ready and take her to her new school the following morning — no matter how sick I was.

At 3.30am, I woke from a fitful sleep in such pain that I could hardly breathe. I rang a button and asked a nurse for pain relief. The next thing I knew, a male doctor was slapping my face hard and saying 'Wake up, stay with me.'

An alarm was ringing. The sound of people running from all directions filled the corridor.

I remember thinking rather dreamily: 'Oh dear, someone must have been taken ill.'

Another doctor felt the pulse in my neck and said: 'She's tachycardic.' I knew this meant an uneven heartbeat — then I realized that the sick person was me. My bed was raced down the corridor by a team of doctors. I was hauled into the operating theatre, and by then I was in so much pain that I was gasping. Then my pulse stopped.

I felt my entire body being sucked up into a white light above.

I remained strangely aware of everything around me. All hell broke loose. I remember the entire medical team swearing. I looked up at the huge, bright-white light above my head, and fought to stay calm as I thought of my three children, who were back home asleep, unaware that Mummy was dying. I remember thinking: 'By the time they wake up, I'll be gone.'

I thought of Ray trying to tell them the bad news. I thought of little blond Charlie, who loved kisses on his cheeks, and I sent him a silent message. 'Goodbye little boy, you'll make someone a lovely husband one day.' I thought of his twin, Archie. 'I hope they tell you what a Mummy's boy you were, and how you used to cry whenever I left the room.'

Then I thought of Ruby with her huge brown eyes and dreamy smile. 'Be a good girl for Daddy and look after the boys. I so wanted to see you grow up.' Death was beckoning but I was aware of everything around me. Suddenly, I felt my entire body being sucked up into the white light above. I found myself in a white tunnel — and I knew I had died. Away from the cursing of the medics and the bleeps of the machines, there was a wonderful sense of calm.

Instead of awful pain, I felt light and clear-headed. I knew what was happening but I felt no fear.

I knew I had to join my loved ones who were already on the other side. It was a tranquil and warm acceptance.

But I also became aware of somebody standing a few feet away from me. I turned, expecting to see my grandmother, who had passed away some years earlier. Instead, it was Ruby — wearing her new school uniform and with her hair tied neatly in bunches.

I was pleased but mildly surprised. I'd never seen her in her uniform, and she'd never allowed me to put her hair in bunches. She smiled and took my hand. 'Come with me, Mummy,' she implored.

I followed her down the white tunnel. She kept turning to check that I was behind her. 'Quick Mummy,' she urged.

At the end stood a gate. I stopped, feeling an urge to walk back down the tunnel, where I was sure my beloved grandmother and other family members who'd passed away would be waiting to greet me.

But little Ruby was insistent. 'Mummy, step through the gates NOW!' Her urgency bought me to my senses. I stepped through it and Ruby slammed it shut behind me.

The shock jolted my body — and I am sure it was at this moment that the defibrillator pads being used by the medics shocked my heart back into a rhythm.

I remember nothing else until I woke up in intensive care. A masked doctor leant over me and said: 'I'm sorry, but you are very sick and you're not out of the woods yet. We need your next of kin at your bedside.'
Again, I thought of little Ruby and her first day at school, and I waved him away.

Somehow, thanks to the experience of travelling through that strange white tunnel, I knew I would be OK. Hours later, Ray arrived at the hospital, bringing with him a photograph of Ruby he'd taken outside the school gates.

She was smiling proudly, with her new uniform and shiny shoes on. But what drew me to the picture was her hair. She had allowed her father to put her hair in bunches for the very first time. This was Ruby exactly as I had seen her in the white tunnel.

I left hospital a week later, after a five-pint blood transfusion. The effects of the surgery were devastating. We were never able to have our much-wanted fourth baby. I lost two stone in weight and couldn't walk properly for months, the blood loss had left me exhausted and anemic. I had a huge scar running down my stomach. And as I was a freelance writer, we struggled financially for many months. But ironically my 'death' was to prove the turning point in my life.

My focus had always been my children, and having to bid them goodbye made me realize just how much I wanted to remain with them. We'd always had a nanny but now I wanted to be totally hands-on with my children. I wanted to be the one who held Ruby's hand at the school gate.

Also, up until this point, I had spent my life worrying about what other people thought of me. As I recovered, I made a pledge that half-friendships and fair-weather friends were no longer enough. I stopped seeing the people I didn't truly love — and told the ones I did just how much they meant to me.

Ray and I had been married for nine years by then, and my experience reminded me that there was nobody else on Earth I wanted to be with. We'd always been devoted to each other but now we both realized just how lost we would be without each other.

Two years after my surgery, I had found new friends, moved my family to a new house, and taken a significant pay cut so I could devote myself to cooking tea and managing every school run, never forgetting for a moment just how lucky I was.

After another year, I was fighting back tears of real emotion as I took the twins to school for their first day.

They complained when I took photo after photo — but it meant so much to me that I was actually there.
I will never be able to understand or explain what happened to me on that fateful day nine years ago. But I no longer harbor a fear about death. And at the same time, I have stopped being scared of life. I've never looked back since.

I am not going to spend a great deal of time on Near Death Experiences, because the objective of this book is not to give you a comfortable piece of evidence to reassure you. The goal is for you to let go of the fear being generated by your ego and live fully in the now. However, as a closing section for this chapter I will reveal that as a part of my research for this book, I spent a lot of time on nursing forums trying to find out what the professionals who witness death on a daily basis have learnt from their experiences. There does appear to be several common themes around the behavior of terminally ill patients in the twenty fours hour prior to their death. Most significant, is an apparent reaching out for something or someone. Palliative care nurses report that, quite often the patient either states that someone (unseen to the nurse) has arrived and wants them to take their hand or they physically reach up from their sick bed as though trying to accept a helping hand up.

Secondly there seems to be a frequently recurring insistence from the dying individual that they are going on a trip. Death bed patients are often reported asking for their passport or a suitcase, when the nurse or relative enquires as to why they need such things (it should be more than obvious that they are going nowhere), they appear confused at the question. It is as though the enquirer should be aware of the impending journey. Perhaps most significantly, there are very few reports of dying individuals in a state of terror or dread. When it comes to the thing we fear the most, it would appear peacefulness (experienced by 90% of people in a NDE) and being wrapped in a white loving light (experienced by 77%) are the overriding sensations.

Chapter Eight – Dying Before Your Death

"Many people die at twenty-five and aren't buried until they are seventy-five." Benjamin Franklin

I hope that what you have read so far makes sense, but no doubt you are wondering how you can take this knowledge and make it a part of who you are. It's all very well agreeing that we shouldn't be afraid of death, but how do we make that our reality?

You are not going to get a say when it's your turn to go. It could be today; it could be in fifty years' time or at any point in between. Life turns on a dime as they say, the 2977 innocent people who died in the attacks on the twin towers, all had plans for September 12th. If you want to really embed this knowledge and learn from what happened that fateful day, go visit ground zero in New York. What you will see there, are the names of the thousands of individuals who died that day. Inside the national 9/11 museum you will hear the phone calls that passengers on the planes made to their family in the moments before they died. No doubt you have heard the over used saying of 'live everyday like it is your last'. It seems like everyone agrees that this is a good motto to have and certainly if Facebook was reality, then we would appear to be all living this policy on a daily basis. Sadly, social media is all mouth and no trousers. You find just as many hypocrites on Facebook as you will find in church.

What 'living each day as though its your last' almost certainly does not mean, is to go crazy and have the party of your life. If you knew in advance at what point you would die, I would assume that most people would get their affairs in order, try to look after the loved ones they are leaving behind and go out as peacefully and prepared as possible. You would have had sufficient time to go through the five stages of grieving and reach the end stage of acceptance. Acceptance of your death means that you are no longer in denial or angry about it. You no longer try and make deals with God or get depressed thinking about it, you are at peace. Essentially you have died before your death, and that is the objective of 'Infinity'.

I always try to conclude my books with easy to follow action points that you can implement quickly and easily into your life. I do this because I have read hundreds of self-help and personal development books where I get to the end and think 'and now what am I supposed to do'?

Here are the steps that I suggest you take, starting today:

Make Peace

Make peace with whomever you need to (including yourself). Do you have a long unresolved argument with someone? Then make it right today (not tomorrow).

In 2009 a palliative care nurse by the name of Bronnie Ware, wrote a short blog post on the five most common regrets of terminally ill patients who were about to die. Bronnie based her essay, on what the many hundreds of people she had witnessed on their death beds over the years of her nursing career, had told her in the hours and minutes before they died. Her revelations took the internet and new thought authors such as myself by storm and she has since published a bestselling book called 'The Top 5 Regrets of The Dying'. Here are the five most common regrets she discovered:

1. **I wish I'd had the courage to live a life true to myself, not the life others expected of me.**

"This was the most common regret of all. When people realize that their life is almost over and look back clearly on it, it is easy to see how many dreams have gone unfulfilled. Most people had not honored even a half of their dreams and had to die knowing that it was due to choices they had made, or not made. Health brings a freedom very few realize, until they no longer have it."

2. **I wish I hadn't worked so hard.**

"This came from every male patient that I nursed. They missed their children's youth and their partner's companionship. Women also spoke of this regret, but as most were from an older generation, many of the female patients had not been breadwinners. All of the men I nursed deeply regretted spending so much of their lives on the treadmill of a work existence."

3. **I wish I'd had the courage to express my feelings.**

"Many people suppressed their feelings in order to keep peace with others. As a result, they settled for a mediocre existence and never became who they were truly capable of becoming. Many developed illnesses relating to the bitterness and resentment they carried as a result."

4. I wish I had stayed in touch with my friends.

"Often they would not truly realize the full benefits of old friends until their dying weeks and it was not always possible to track them down. Many had become so caught up in their own lives that they had let golden friendships slip by over the years. There were many deep regrets about not giving friendships the time and effort that they deserved. Everyone misses their friends when they are dying."

5. I wish that I had let myself be happier.

"This is a surprisingly common one. Many did not realize until the end that happiness is a choice. They had stayed stuck in old patterns and habits. The so-called 'comfort' of familiarity overflowed into their emotions, as well as their physical lives. Fear of change had them pretending to others, and to their selves, that they were content, when deep within, they longed to laugh properly and have silliness in their life again."

You will notice that nowhere in the top five is there anything like 'I wish I had bought more property' or 'I wish I had had a better car'. The regrets at the end of life are all to do with state of mind, love and relationships. All temporary and transient things that cannot be owned or stored away in a bank vault.

Embrace the Temporary

I had a friend once called Mike, the thing that everyone knew about Mike was he lives entirely for the weekend. He works on a production line in a processed meat packing factory and he hates every second of his day at work. On a Monday he starts talking about his plans for the weekend and when Friday comes he is the happiest man on planet earth – he goes wild for 48 hours. On a Sunday he tries to stay up as late as he possibly can, why? Because he knows that as soon as he closes his eyes and falls asleep, it becomes Monday again. I don't know what Mike is doing now, but I do know that if he is still living the same way then he is not happy. Mike wants the impossible; he wants to make the weekend permanent – that can never happen!

Try to become aware of the temporariness of everything. If you have a beautiful meal, savor every moment of it and notice that it comes to an end. When you go on vacation, pay as much attention to the end as you did to the start. Become as conscious of the temporary as you can, embrace it and see it everywhere – because that is exactly what it is, everywhere and in everything!

Tell Them You Love Them

My Granddad Jack died before I told him how much of a hero he had been to me. I never told him just how much I loved him because I assumed he would always be there.

Make sure that when you say goodbye to people on a daily basis, you say it with conviction and love. Did you tell your partner, your children, your mother and your father that you loved them today? You may look back one day and wish you had used that four-letter word with someone much more than you did!

Stop Taking Money So Seriously

I have a friend who is like Scrooge McDuck. I have never known anyone as afraid to spend money as this guy. He even takes toilet roll from work so he doesn't have to buy it. I have no idea how much money he has in the bank, but it must be a considerable amount because I have never seen him break anything bigger than a $20 bill. I told him recently that I hope I get an invite to his funeral because he is going to have the most lavish, jewel incrusted coffin the world has ever seen. He wasn't very happy at that suggestion, but I am still not sure if he was offended at talk of his demise or the fact that he might one day be forced to spend some money.

We take money far too seriously when in reality it's just something we invented to save time. Before money, buying things involved a lot of debate and bartering. As Alan Watts says "It is absurd to take money too seriously, to confuse it with real wealth, because it will do you no good to eat it or wear it for clothing. Money is more or less static, for gold, silver, strong paper or a bank balance can "stay put" for a long time. But real wealth, such as food, is perishable. Thus, a community may possess all the gold in the world, but if it does not farm its crops it will starve".

I am not saying you should go blow all your money on expensive material things, for such an action serves just as little purpose as hoarding money does. Money gives you the power to improve the lives of others and once you let go of the need to store it as an illusionary safety blanket, the universe will find ways for you to help others! On your death bed, the Bentley on your drive or the Rolex on your wrist are likely to be nothing but irrelevant trinkets to you. However, a lifetime of making a difference to other people is apt to bring even more peace to your final moments.

Start Listening to The Primary Thought Event

Have you ever driven past someone broken down on the hard shoulder of the highway? Perhaps an elderly gentleman or a young mother with a couple of children in the back seat. You consider pulling over to help her but think better of it and drive on. You feel a little guilty for a while and so you turn the radio up to drown out the sounds of your pesky conscience. The voice that said help, is your primary thought and the voice that said keep driving, is your ego. This opinion of the ego is always a 'Secondary Thought Event', in other words, whilst you come to these judgments in the blink of an eye, faster than any modern day computer, they still cross the finishing line into your mind in a clear second place. There is a thought that comes half a second before these opinions, and this is what I call 'The Primary Thought Event (PTE)'.

Normally PTE's happen around questions of integrity and so you are unlikely to feel their presence whilst trying to decide what flavor ice cream to buy at the movie theatre, or which pair of shoes to wear on a night out at an expensive restaurant. However, in circumstances of merit this voice resonates throughout your body with clear direction as to what you should do. Actually it is never a voice but rather a feeling and they are easy to identify. But the problem is, you never get much chance to analyze the sensation and be fully aware of what it is. The ego is in high pursuit behind the PTE and will arrive in your mind within half a second. In most cases, the first thing your ego will do is to try and prevent you taking any action based on that primary thought. It strongly and convincingly argues that you should ignore the primary thought event completely.

Why does the conscious fear this voice so much? Because it shatters the illusion that the ego has spent a lifetime trying to convince you is real. The ego hates any reminder that it is not in control of your destiny. The Primary Thought Event is the voice of your soul. It comes from a position of pure love and is blessed with the knowledge and understanding of what this life is all about. It knows that you have nothing to lose and it knows there is no such thing as death. It knows what is best for you and given half the chance, it would steer you on the path that serves you best. However, the ego will fight hard to prevent this disaster from happening, because it knows this source has no attachment to anything material. It is highly likely to suggest that you give away a raft of things your ego has spent many years persuading you to acquire.

Your conscious mind will tell you that your home is your castle and nobody can take it off you. It will tell you that you have a better car than your neighbor and as such must be more successful. The ego will tell you that your marriage will last forever and a million other things that hint at permanency being possible. It does this, not for your benefit, but out of an insane drive to defy the unbreakable law of mortality. It tries to build a world where things can last forever in the hope that if it can make that concept true, then it will one day also be able to avoid the inevitable.

Let me paint a picture for you, a typical example of the PTE being ignored... A city worker pushed open the thick glass door of his air-conditioned office and walked out into the warm muggy air of the busy street. His expensive suit cuts him a fine and respectable figure as he walks to the nearby deli to pick up a sandwich and orange juice for his lunch. On route, no more than fifty meters from his office door, he spots a young man slumped on the floor, begging for loose change. He must be no more than 19 years old, his clothes are dirty and torn and he has an expression of hopelessness etched into his young face. He is not bothering people, just simply holding out a scrawny, limp and defeated hand for any coins. BANG! A PTE happens that clearly says 'give the man money, give him lots of money', it says to the city gent 'you have plenty, even if you emptied all the notes from your wallet it wouldn't make any difference you would just refill the wallet from the abundance that you have'. This opinion represents who you are at a divine level, it is the voice of your soul, or if you want a more grandiose statement, this is the voice of God. Less than half a second later, his ego goes into panic at the thought that he might actually be considering 'giving this person all our money'.

The ego, with a scarcity mindset, has alarm bells ringing all over the place and it begins to argue that it would be ridiculous to give all the money to this man, because then there wouldn't be enough left to buy lunch. As he gets closer to the homeless man, his mind is in turmoil. He feels that he should give the man money, but can't argue against the strong position of the conscious mind. The ego suggests a compromise; maybe just a few coins would be better and more appropriate than the folding stuff. Desperately the man hunts in his pocket for loose change. He can't find any and his ego advises to avoid looking bad, so he simply crosses the road to skip the situation altogether.

So the man crosses the road and continues his journey to the sandwich shop, the down and out who really needed the money got nothing, and the gentleman who was talked out of responding to the PTE, lost the opportunity to experience the joy of giving to another and flowing in the same direction as his soul.

Did the city worker do a bad thing? No. As we have previously stated, good and bad are always subjective, the homeless man may have used that money to clean himself up and eat a decent meal, or he could just have likely spent it on alcohol or hard drugs. No act is either good or bad, but rather it is a decision that either serves us or it doesn't serve us.

When you follow the PTE, you allow perfection to flow into your life, it's the gift that keeps giving. The person you helped benefits (although this is almost irrelevant), you also benefit by doing something that 'serves you' and your act of choosing to permit divinity to act in defiance of the ego, causes disruption to the power of the conscious mind. Every time the ego is prevented from controlling your response to life's events, it gets a fraction of a percent weaker as a result.

Collect Memories Not Things

Experiences are temporary and that is what makes them so beautiful. Come the day you die all the 'stuff' you collected won't make the slightest difference to you. They won't make you happier; they won't make you sad either. They will simply be an irrelevance. If you spend your time accumulating 'things', then you are dedicating your life to building something that doesn't mean anything. Imagine for me, that on your deathbed a genie appeared and offered you an extra month alive, in return for your car and your watch. I would imagine most people would take the deal. But imagine if the genie wanted your memories of the day your son was born and the day you married your soul mate, no deal right?

The point of life is to be alive, and nothing more than that; trust me on this, you will go out the same way you came in. You will take nothing with you, not even the clothes on your back. Be alive now, not tomorrow, not when you have lost a bit of weight, not when you get the promotion at work. This moment right now is all there will ever be - so make it count.

Thank you for reading 'Infinity'. I sincerely hope the knowledge you have gained here, makes the same huge and dramatic difference to your life that originally happened to me. If you would like to be the first to get my newly released books and audiobooks, go to www.CraigBeck.com and join my VIP newsletter. I always give away 50 free copies of each new audiobook release to members of the list, so check the box to let me know you want to be entered into the draw.

As a final closing favour for me, if you have enjoyed this book would you please help me spread the word of this life enhancing principle, by writing a review on Amazon, Audible or whichever online store you purchased it from. I always read the reviews and they really mean a great deal to me. Remember the future does not exist, so please make me smile and go do it now!

Until we speak again, peace and love.

Craig Beck

Ps. I spoke about animals quite a lot in this book. If you have the space, time and commitment to give an animal a loving home, then please visit your local rescue shelter first. There are thousands of beautiful cats and dogs who are desperate for a second chance. I can tell you from experience that they will give you more love than you ever thought possible.

Also available from Craig Beck

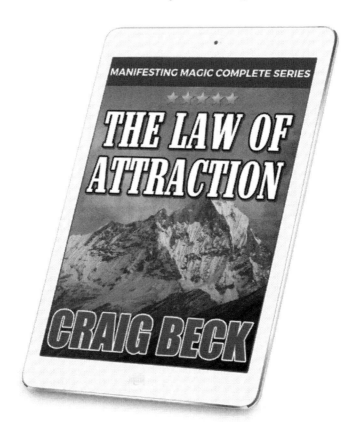

The Law of Attraction can easily be understood by becoming aware that 'like attracts like' or putting it another way 'you get back what you give out'. Sounds simple, but how do you make it an automatic part of your being?

An essential component of the Law of Attraction is realizing that where you fix your attention can have a powerful impact on what happens to you. However, despite what you may have been told, your ability to manifest the life of your dreams has nothing to do with positive thinking and affirmations. Think anything you want but unless you believe it, you will not be sending the right vibrations out into the universe to have it appear.

You see, everything in the world is just energy vibrating at different frequencies. The sports car you want is just the same as you, a collection of atomic particles fluctuating at a precise frequency to generate it's physical form. If you want the sports car in your life, you simply have to send out the intention resonating at the exact same frequency.

You may be wondering if this is all true then why do so many people continue to suffer with poverty, lack and want. Most people simply dismiss this theory as 'new age mumbo jumbo', but this is a law and just like any other it doesn't care whether you believe or not. The law of gravity applies its force on you regardless of what you believe and so does the law of attraction.

Even though there is a great deal of value to even merely finding out what the Law of Attraction is, this profound book takes you to an advanced level of understanding. In short, if you implement everything you read in this book your life will change more positively and dramatically than you may have ever believed possible.

You will come to be more attentive to underlying negativity and can begin to combat it with new beliefs and sensations that better reflect your constructive vision of the upcoming future. This ongoing focus on self-reflection also allows you to start seeing what you really want from your life, and you can then advance to developing clearer objectives with actionable steps at every stage.

Broken down into seven powerful chapters, each dealing with an important area of your life. This book has the power to deliver the life of your dreams but remember whether you believe that claim or not, you are right! If you can open your mind to a concept that has already changed the lives of thousands then you have truly found the genie's lamp!

- How to attract money using the law of attraction
- Living in abundance
- Find your soul mate and more love than you thought possible
- Manifest perfect health and vitality
- Ask believe receive
- Becoming fearless

www.craigbeck.com

Printed in Great Britain
by Amazon